CHECK-MATE

A POCKET-SIZE GUIDE TO EVERYDAY SPELLINGS FOR DYSLEXICS

D1613275

of related interest

Dyslexia
How Would I Cope?
2nd edition
Michael V Ryden
ISBN 1 85302 154 7 64 pages

'Written from personal experience, this book
clearly describes and illustrates how written
communication can appear to a dyslexic
person.'

– *Disabled Living Foundation*

CHECK-MATE

A POCKET-SIZE GUIDE TO EVERYDAY SPELLINGS FOR DYSLEXICS

Alan O'Brien

Jessica Kingsley Publishers
London and Philadelphia

First published in the United Kingdom in 1993 by
Jessica Kingsley Publishers Ltd
116 Pentonville Road
London N1 9JB

Copyright © 1993 Alan O'Brien

British Library Cataloguing in Publication Data
O'Brien, Alan
Check-mate: Pocket Size Guide to Everyday
Spellings for Dyslexics
I. Title
428.1
ISBN 1 85302 165 2

Printed and Bound in Great Britain by
Cromwell Press, Melksham, Wiltshire

CONTENTS

ACKNOWLEDGEMENTS

A special thank you to Elaine Love and Jessica, Helen, Charlotte and Anna at Jessica Kingsley Publishers.

FOREWORD

When Alan O'Brien first contacted me to discuss publication of CHECK-MATE, his pocket-size guide to everyday spellings for dyslexics, it seemed to me that he had a good idea.

As always, personal experience of problems leads to effective solutions.

Alan's own experience as a dyslexic who lacked confidence in putting pen to paper is very common. Fortunately, his determination to overcome his difficulties led him to devise a support system which would give him the confidence to tackle problems as they arose. He is now sharing his system with others.

Most dyslexics experience difficulties in organising their own learning. It is valuable therefore to remember that in the same way that there is a group of words which is most commonly used by us all, there are specific pieces of information and associated words which are essential to everyday living. CHECK-MATE addressed this basic information and provides a 'survival kit' for the user.

I use my Filofax as a working tool in organising my life; it is tagged with 'Post-it' stickers and notes. It would be good to see CHECK-MATE being used in the same way and being made personal as an aid to developing strategy in overcoming the individual owner's needs. If it can be used like this, and be kept at hand for regular reference, it should prove an invaluable aid.

Liz Brooks
Executive Director
The Dyslexic Institute

INTRODUCTION

Have you ever felt fairly sure that you know how to spell something, but haven't had the confidence actually to take the plunge and commit pen to paper?

Being a dyslexic, I've often found myself in this position, whether it be uncertainty about how to spell 'Happy' in a birthday card, or how to write the amount £40 in words when writing a cheque. Even as a child, although I had not been diagnosed as being dyslexic, I knew I had problems with spelling and refused to join the rest of my peers in writing graffiti on walls in case I spelt it wrong!

This is where this book comes in. I have listed spellings and other useful information to cover most of the situations in which I have found myself unable to get round my bad spelling. Obviously, a telephone call can, in a lot of instances, replace written messages, but what happens when you really have to write something down?

Instead of getting into a panic where the mere thought of looking up a word in a dictionary makes you break out in a cold sweat, look first of all in this book. I've listed such things as how to write numbers in words, messages commonly used on greetings cards, and many more words and useful phrases.

Keep *Check-Mate* with you as you would a diary, and you have the reassurance that when you want a word, you can check it here with the minimum of fuss and embarrassment. There is also a space at the end for you to note down specific words that you find you need to use regularly.

WHAT TO LOOK FOR IF YOU SUSPECT YOUR CHILD MAY BE DYSLEXIC

- Slow to crawl as a baby, unable to crawl, or unco-ordinated when attempting to crawl
- Bed-wetting up to the age of 4 or 5
- Slow to distinguish left from right
- Difficulty in learning how to tie shoe laces, do up coat etc.
- Writing numbers and letters back to front
- Poor concentration span
- Reading: may not see the first letter of a word, or may incorporate letters from the line underneath into the word they are trying to read
- Poor memory.

There is now a lot of help that can be given to children with dyslexia in areas such as reading and writing.

HELPFUL HINTS

- Try to read as much as possible – it may be easiest to start off with children's books. If you have children, reading them a bed-time story will give you a good excuse – you can read the story through to yourself during the day in preparation.

- If you have to pay a bill by cheque over the counter at the Post Office or at a showroom, write out the cheque before you go. There are usually instructions on the back of the bill as to who to make the cheque out to so that you can follow the correct spelling.

- Investigate the adult literacy classes available in your area. These are usually held at a college of further education and may well help you – why not give them a call?

- If you suspect that you are dyslexic or that your child suffers from dyslexia, consult the Dyslexia Association – the address and telephone number is listed at the back of the book. Also, look in your local library to see if there are any local dyslexia associations which may be able to offer you support and advice.

THE ALPHABET

A	B	C	D	E	F	G
a	b	c	d	e	f	g

H	I	J	K	L	M
h	i	j	k	l	m

N	O	P	Q	R	S	T
n	o	p	q	r	s	t

U	V	W	X	Y	Z
u	v	w	x	y	z

NUMBERS

0	zero	15	fifteen
1	one	16	sixteen
2	two	17	seventeen
3	three	18	eighteen
4	four	19	nineteen
5	five	20	twenty
6	six		
7	seven	30	thirty
8	eight	40	forty
9	nine	50	fifty
10	ten	60	sixty
11	eleven	70	seventy
12	twelve	80	eighty
13	thirteen	90	ninety
14	fourteen	100	one hundred

1000	one thousand
1,000,000	one million
250,000	two hundred and fifty thousand (a quarter of a million)
500,000	five hundred thousand (half a million)

$\frac{1}{2}$	half		$10\frac{1}{2}$	ten and a half
$\frac{1}{4}$	a quarter
$\frac{3}{4}$	three quarters
$\frac{1}{3}$	a third
$\frac{2}{3}$	two thirds

CURRENCY

£	pounds	¥	yen
p	pence	$	dollars
Dm	deutschmark

DATES AND DAYS

1st	first	13th	thirteenth
2nd	second	14th	fourteenth
3rd	third	15th	fifteenth
4th	fourth	16th	sixteenth
5th	fifth	17th	seventeenth
6th	sixth	18th	eighteenth
7th	seventh	19th	nineteenth
8th	eighth	20th	twentieth
9th	ninth	21st	twenty-first
10th	tenth	30th	thirtieth
11th	eleventh	31st	thirty-first
12th	twelfth		

Monday	Friday
Tuesday	Saturday
Wednesday	Sunday
Thursday	

MONTHS

January	July
February	August
March	September
April	October
May	November
June	December

WORD LIST

today	second	morning
tomorrow	minute	afternoon
yesterday	hour	evening
week	o'clock	day
weekend	quarter to	night
fortnight	quarter past	noon
month	half-past	midday
year	next	midnight
decade	last	
century		

COLOURS

beige	gold	pink	white
black	green	purple	yellow
blue	grey	red	
bronze	orange	silver	
brown	mauve	turquoise	

dark	bright	pale

CLOTHES

belt	jumper	socks
blazer	pants	suit
boots	leggings	sweatshirt
cardigan	scarf	tie
coat	shirt	trainers
dress	skirt	trousers
jacket	shoes	underpants
jeans	shorts	vest
jersey	skirt	waistcoat

THE BANK

Please send me a new cheque book
Please send me a statement of my account
Please transfer £... to my ... account
Please credit the enclosed cheque for ...
   to my ... account
Please send me a list of standing orders/
   direct debits

£ pound(s)	insurance
p pence	interest rate
A/C payee only	loan
account	mortgage
bank charges	only
cancelled	overdraft
cash	rate
cashier	repayment
chequebook	self
credit	service card
current	standing order
deposit	statement
direct debit	transfer
facility	

WELFARE

I enclose my application form for ...
Please confirm that ...

advice	form
allowance	housing
apply for	husband
benefit	income support
children	maternity
council	mobility
councillor	office
credit	payment
deduction	service
department	sickness
disability	social security
education	unemplyment
family	wife

HEALTH

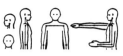

ache
allergy
antibiotics
appointment
aspirin
asthma
blood
bronchitis
chicken pox
complaint
cough
dentist
diabetes
diarrhoea
doctor
eczema
filling
flu
German measles

heart
hospital
injection
measles
mumps
operation
optician
paracetamol
prescription
sample
specialist
stomach
surgery
throat
tonsillitis
unwell
urine
vaccination

SPORT

aerobics	football	skiing
athletics	gymnastics	soccer
badminton	hockey	squash
baseball	rowing	swimming
basketball	rugby	tennis
cricket	sailing	weights

ball	ground	pitch
court	kit	racquet

away	match	score
competition	opponent	set
fixture	partner	stopwatch
game	point	time
goal	race	training
home	referee	umpire

TRAVEL

Having a lovely time – wish you were here!

airport	drink	scenery
apartment	flight	sea
arrived safely	food	sunburn
awful	friends	ticket
beach	holiday	tour
beautiful	hotel	train
camp site	insurance	traveller's cheques
cancelled	journey	vaccination
coach	local	view
complain	luggage	visa
currency	passport	weather
customs	plane	wonderful
delayed	rescheduled	
discotheque	sand	

WORD LIST

WORDS WHICH CONTAIN SILENT LETTERS

silent 'b'

bomb	debtor	numb
climb	doubt	plumber
comb	dumb	thumb
crumb	lamb	tomb
debt	limb	

silent 'g'

consignment	gnat	phlegm
design	gnome	resign
diaphragm	neighbour	signpost
foreigner	night	sleigh

silent 'p'

pneumatic	psalm	psychology
pneumonia	pseudomym	receipt

silent 'k'

knack	knelt	knock
knave	knife	knot
knead	knight	know
knee	knit	knowledge
kneel	knob	knuckle

silent 'w'

wrangle	wrench	wrinkle
wrap	wrestle	wrist
wreath	wretch	write
wreck	wriggle	writing
wren	wring	wrong

SHOPPING LIST

Copy brand names and product names from tins and packets that you may have in your cupboards. The following are some basics:

General

detergent	magazine	video
disinfectant	newspaper	vitamin pills
floor cleaner	soap powder	washing-up liquid

Groceries

biscuits	herbs	rolls
bread	jam	salt
cake	loaf	sliced
cereal	marmalade	sugar
coffee	pasta	tea
flour	pepper	wheatmeal
granary	rice	wholemeal

Drinks

beer	lager	tonic water
cola	lemonade	vodka
fruit juice	mineral water	whisky
gin	soda water	wine

Dairy

butter	eggs	pint
cheese	free-range	single
cream	half	skimmed
double	low-fat	whipped
dozen	milk	yoghurt

Meat and poultry

bacon	fillet	liver
beef	ham	mince
breast	joint	pork
burger	kidney	roast
chicken	lamb	sausages
chops	leg	veal

Fish

cockles	mussels	shrimp
cod	plaice	smoked
haddock	prawn	squid
hake	salmon	trout
mackerel	scampi	tuna

Vegetables

beetroot	cucumber	peas
beans	leek	potato
cabbage	lettuce	spinach
carrot	mushroom	sweetcorn
cauliflower	onion	tomato
courgette	parsnip	turnip

Fruit

apple	grapefruit	peach
apricot	lemon	plum
avocado	melon	raspberry
banana	nectarine	satsuma
blackberry	orange	strawberry
grape	pear	tangerine

Toiletries

antiseptic	flannel	soap
after shave	hairbrush	sponge
bubble bath	lotion	talcum powder
comb	razor	toilet roll
conditioner	razor blades	toothbrush
deodorant	shampoo	toothpaste
elastoplast	shaving foam	

MESSAGES

MILKMAN

No milk today/until next Saturday/
tomorrow, thank you.

One extra pint today, please.

Please leave cream/orange
juice/eggs/bread/cheese

POSTMAN

Please leave delivery/deliveries next door
at Number 6/in the garage/at the back
door/in the shed.

Beware of the dog

Not at this address

Gone away

Return to sender

THE CAR

Most of the spellings you need will be listed in your car manual but here are the basics:

Please would you check

battery	engine	mirror
back	exhaust	petrol/fuel
electrics	oil	pipe
brakes	front	points
bulb	gears	radiator
carburettor	handbrake	tracking
choke	headlights	tyre pressure
clutch	indicators	tyres

Tax in post
On tow
Broken down
Back in 5 minutes
Gone for petrol
Running in – please pass
Permit applied for
For sale £ ..., please ring

OTHERS

Called – got no reply

Keep off the grass

Out for lunch, back in 10 minutes

Please make another appointment

Please mind the step

Please put newspapers through the letter box

Wet concrete

Wet paint on door/frame/window/step

Broken glass	Private
Closed	Thank you
Fragile	Wipe your feet
Please	With care

GREETINGS

Happy

Birthday
Christmas
Easter
New Year
Diwali
Chanakah
Passover
Ramadan
Baisahki

Wishing you all
the best in

the future
your retirement
your new home / job

Thank you

for all your help
for your hospitality
for having me
for a lovely evening

Congratulations on	passing your driving test
	your promotion
	passing your exams
	your marriage
	your engagement
	the birth of your baby son/daughter
	your eighteenth birthday
Sorry	it's late
	to hear you're not feeling well/you've been ill
	you're leaving
	to hear of your sad loss

Thinking of you

Write soon

Look forward to hearing from you

Best wishes

Good luck

Lots of love

All good wishes to you and your family

Sincere condolences

from

Many happy returns of the day

Bon voyage

Well done

FAMILY MEMBERS

Mother
  Mum
  Mummy
	Father
	  Dad
	  Daddy

Sister	Brother
Aunt Auntie	Uncle

Grandmother
  Gran
  Grandma
  Granny
  Nan
	Grandfather
	  Grandpa
	  Grandad

Niece	Nephew
Cousin	Great

TELEPHONE MESSAGES

When you take a telephone message for someone try not to get bogged down by agreeing to pass on a long message. The information you should take, however, is:

. The name of the caller
. The name of the organisation or company they represent
. The telephone number
. The time of the call
. When or whether they would like their call returned.

Don't be nervous about asking people to spell their names out. It is common practice when using the telephone, as words often become distorted and indistinct.

If you are take messages regularly, there are telephone message pads which you can use, where you can tick a box to indicate information.

USEFUL WORDS AND PHRASES

phoned

called

this morning/afternoon/evening

please call back

today/tomorrow

urgent

he/she will call you back later

at the office

at work

at home

he/she will be at

Called while you were out

will be away until

LETTERS

Always remember to put your full address at the top of the letter you are writing. If you write letters regularly, it may be an idea to order a batch of small self-adhesive labels pre-printed with your name, address and telephone number. When signing a letter, be sure to print your name underneath – not everyone will be able to make out your name from your signature.

SCHOOL

Dear ………

(NAME) was unable to attend school on …… as he/she was ill with a stomach upset/flu/bad cold

OR

Please excuse …………… from swimming/games, for the rest of this week/today as he/she has a cold.

OR

(NAME) will be absent from school on (DAY) morning/afternoon as he has a hospital appointment at 3 o'clock.

Yours sincerely

SAMPLE REPLY LETTERS

Dear Sirs

I am interested in ...... as mentioned/advertised in this week's ...... Please would you send me a brochure or any other literature you may have. I enclose a stamped, addressed envelope.

Yours truly

Dear Sirs

I am writing in response to your advertisement in the ...... for ....

I would like to place an order and enclose my cheque/postal order to cover the cost, including postage and packing.

Yours truly

JOB APPLICATIONS

Filling in job application forms can be a long exercise. However, it can be made easier if you compile a CV (curriculum vitae). This is a listing of personal details, education and qualifications and a listing of jobs in date order with a brief description. Once you have drawn up you CV, it can be added to and updated each time you change a job. There are many typing agencies who can type your CV for you. They have experience in laying out the information so that it is easily readable, and they should also check any spelling. They will charge a fee for this service, but it is well worth while, as you can copy any or all of the information onto an application form.

If you have to complete a job application form, ask a friend or member of your family to check it through before sending it off. Any mistakes in spelling or grammar may hinder your chances of getting the all-important interview. If your handwriting is bad you can type the information.

Once you get an interview, be confident. Most dyslexics are very good at expressing themselves verbally and this is your chance to shine.

It is often best not to say that you are dyslexic either on an application form, or in an interview – it is better to say that you are a terrible speller. Other people, prospective employers included, are not always familiar with the characteristics of dyslexia and may take it to mean that you are of low intelligence. If you do say that you are dyslexic, make sure that you explain exactly what it is and how it affects you (i.e. whether your reading or writing suffers more) and explain what steps you take to overcome the problem. Be sure to explain that dyslexia is not related to intelligence.

The main headings in a CV are:

Name: GIVE FULL NAME

Address:

Telephone no: (INCLUDE THE DIALLING CODE)

Date of birth:

Marital status: Married/Single/
                  Divorced/Separated

Dependants: e.g. Three children aged 3, 6
               and 10/None

Nationality: e.g. British

Education:

Secondary school level and upwards should be listed. Put the name of each institution, the dates you attended and list any qualifications you gained whilst there.

Employment history:

Start with your most recent job and work backwards. Give the starting and leaving dates, the name of the company you worked for and its address. State your job title and give a brief description of what your duties involved.

Other information:

State any experience you have had which may contribute to the job, whether you hold a driving licence or any other information you may think is relevant.

Hobbies and interests:

These can also be listed, together with memberships of any organisations and any positions of authority you hold e.g. Treasurer, Photographic Society.

References:

Give the name and address of at least two people who know you and would be willing to give you a reference. One of these should be a present or past employer.

Replying to a vacancy advertised in a newspaper

Dear Sirs

I have seen your advertisement in today's edition of ...... for a ...... (e.g. warehouse manager).

EITHER

I am interested in applying for this position and I would be grateful if you would send me further details of the vacancy together with an application form.

OR

I would like to apply for the position and am enclosing a copy of my CV for your consideration.

Yours truly

Note: Remember to put your full address at the top of the letter and print your name underneath your signature.

Annual salary

If a salary is quoted p.a. (per annum), to work out weekly pay (before tax) roughly divide by 50:

£8000 p.a. = approximately £160 per week

£9000 p.a. = approximately £180 per week

£10,000 p.a. = approximately £200 per week

£11,000 p.a. = approximately £220 per week

£12,000 p.a. = approximately £240 per week

£15,000 p.a. = approximately £300 per week

£18,000 p.a. = approximately £360 per week

£20,000 p.a. = approximately £400 per week

£25,000 p.a. = approximately £500 per week

£30,000 p.a. = approximately £600 per week

THE 24-HOUR CLOCK

1.00 am	01.00 hours	1.00 pm	13.00 hours
1.15 am	01.15 hours	2.00 pm	14.00 hours
1.30 am	01.30 hours	3.00 pm	15.00 hours
1.45 am	01.45 hours	4.00 pm	16.00 hours
2.00 am	02.00 hours	5.00 pm	17.00 hours
3.00 am	03.00 hours	6.00 pm	18.00 hours
4.00 am	04.00 hours	7.00 pm	19.00 hours
5.00 am	05.00 hours	8.00 pm	20.00 hours
6.00 am	06.00 hours	9.00 pm	21.00 hours
7.00 am	07.00 hours	10.00 pm	22.00 hours
8.00 am	08.00 hours	11.00 pm	23.00 hours
9.00 am	09.00 hours	11.30 pm	23.30 hours
10.00 am	10.00 hours	11.45 pm	23.45 hours
11.00 am	11.00 hours	11.59 pm	23.59 hours
12 noon	12.00 hours		

BUT

12 midnight (which is neither am nor pm)
The international sign is MIDNIGHT. One
minute after midnight is shown as 00.01 hours.

WEIGHTS AND MEASURES

Linear measure

    1 inch = 25.4 millimetres

    1 foot = 12 inches = 0.3048 metres

    1 yard = 3 feet = 0.9144 metres

    1 mile = 1760 yards = 1.609 kilometres

Capacity

    1 pint = 20 fluid ounces = 0.568 litres

    1 quart = 2 pints = 1.136 litres

    1 gallon = 4 quarts = 4.546 litres

Weight

    1 ounce = 28.35 grams

    1 pound = 16 ounces = 0.4536 kilograms

    1 kilo = 1000 grams = 2.205 pounds

    1 stone = 14 pounds = 6.35 kilograms

CONVERSION TABLES

To convert to metric measurements,
multiply the relevant number of miles,
yards etc. by the number in the right
hand column. The figure you get is the
equivalent number of kilometres, metres
etc.

e.g. 4 miles = 4 x 1.6093 = 6.44 kilometres

To convert from metric, divide the
number of kilometres, metres etc. in the
second column by the number in the
right hand column. The answer you get is
the number of miles, yards etc.

e.g. 10 kilometres = 10 x 1.6093 = 6.21 miles

Length

miles : kilometres	x/÷	1.6093
yards : metres	x/÷	0.9144
feet : metres	x/÷	0.3048
inches: centimetres	x/÷	2.5400

Mass

tons : kilograms	x/÷	1016.0500
tons : tonnes	x/÷	1.0160
pounds : kilograms	x/÷	0.4536
ounces : grams	x/÷	28.3495

Capacity

gallons : litres	x/÷	4.5460
pints : litres	x/÷	0.5680

TEMPERATURE

Fahrenheit

Water boils at 212°F and freezes at 32°F

Celsius or Centigrade

Water boils at 100°C and freezes at 0°C

Normal body temperature = 37°C = 98.6°F

Conversion tables

0°F = -17°C	80°F = 27°C
20°F = - 7°C	90°F = 32°C
32°F = 0°C	98°F = 37°C
40°F = 5°C	100°F = 38°C
50°F = 10°C	150°F = 66°C
60°F = 16°C	200°F = 93°C
70°F = 21°C	212°F =100°C

To convert Celsius to Fahrenheit:

multiply °C by 9, divide by 5 and add 32

To convert Fahrenheit to Celsius:

subtract 32, multiply by 5 and divide by 9

PERCENTAGES   %

To work out percentages, for example on 'Sale' signs showing 10% or 20% off marked prices, follow the guide below:

10% = 1/10 (1 tenth)

so: 10% of 10   = 1
      10% of 100   = 10
      10% of 200   = 20 and so on

5% is half of 10% = 1/2 of 10

so: 5% of 10   = 0.5
      5% of 100   = 5
      5% of 200   = 10

so: 15% of £100 = £15
      15% of £200 = £30
      15% of £150 = £22.50

CLOTHING AND SHOE SIZES

Women's coats, suits, dresses and blouses

British	8	10	12	14	16	18	20
American	6	8	10	12	14	16	18
Italian	42	44	46	48	50	52	54
French	38	40	42	44	46	48	50

Women's shoes (a guide only)

British	3	4	5	6	7	8	9
American	$4\frac{1}{2}$	$5\frac{1}{2}$	$6\frac{1}{2}$	$7\frac{1}{2}$	$8\frac{1}{2}$	$9\frac{1}{2}$	$10\frac{1}{2}$
Continental	36	37	38	39	40	41	42

Men's coats, jackets and suits

British	34	36	38	40	42	44
American	34	36	38	40	42	44
Continental	44	46	48	50	52	54

Men's shoes (a guide only)

British	6	7	8	9	10	11
American	7	8	9	10	11	12
Continental	$39\frac{1}{2}$	$40\frac{1}{2}$	$41\frac{1}{2}$	$42\frac{1}{2}$	$43\frac{1}{2}$	$44\frac{1}{2}$

Men's shirts

British	14	$14\frac{1}{2}$	15	$15\frac{1}{2}$	16	$16\frac{1}{2}$	17	$17\frac{1}{2}$
American	14	$14\frac{1}{2}$	15	$15\frac{1}{2}$	16	$16\frac{1}{2}$	17	$17\frac{1}{2}$
Continental	36	37	38	39	40	41	42	43

USEFUL ADDRESSES

The British Dyslexia Association can provide details of local associations and libraries and job centres will also be able to help. Many universities now have departments covering disabilities such as dyslexia and also have access to a great deal of information.

Some organisations may charge you for their services. Do check before you use them.

National

British Dyslexia Association
98 London Road
Reading
Berkshire RG1 5AU   Tel: 0734 – 668271/2

Dyslexia Association of Northern Ireland
39 High Street
Hollywood
County Down   Tel: 0232 – 660111

Scottish Dyslexia Association
  Cakemuir House
  Nenthorn
  Kelso
  Roxburghshire   Tel: 0573 – 24806

The Dyslexia Institute
  133 Gresham Road
  Staines
  Middlesex
  TW18 2AJ   Tel: 0784 – 463851

ADDRESSES

The space below can be used to write out names and addresses that you use often. There is also space to write out the correct spelling of names of family members.

Name: _____

Address: _____

_____

_____

Telephone No: _____

Family Names: _____

_____

Name: _____

Address: _____

_____

_____

Telephone No: _____

Family Names: _____

_____

Name: _____

Address: _____

_____

_____

Telephone No: _____

Family Names: _____

_____

Name: _____

Address: _____

_____

_____

Telephone No: _____

Family Names: _____

_____

Name: _____

Address: _____

_____

_____

Telephone No: _____

Family Names: _____

Name: _____

Address: _____

_____

Telephone No: _____

Family Names: _____

_____

Name: _____

Address: _____

_____

Telephone No: _____

Family Names: _____

_____

Name: _____

Address: _____

_____

Telephone No: _____

Family Names: _____

WORD LIST

List here all the words that you may
need to use on a regular basis.

WORD LIST

WORD LIST

WORD LIST

WORD LIST